21
SUPER SIMPLE
Biology
EXPERIMENTS

Rebecca W. Keller, Ph.D

Illustrations: Janet Moneymaker
                 Rebecca W. Keller, PhD

21 Super Simple Biology Experiments
ISBN 978-1-936114-07-8

Published by Gravitas Publications, Inc.
www.gravitaspublications.com

Printed in United States

What Are Super Simple Science Experiments?

Super Simple Science Experiments are experiments that each focus on one aspect of scientific investigation. Doing science requires students to develop different types of skills. These skills include the ability to make good observations, to turn observations into questions and/or hypotheses, to build and use models, to analyze data, to use controls, and to use a variety of science tools including computers.

Super Simple Science Experiments breaks down the steps of scientific investigation so that students can focus on one aspect of scientific inquiry at a time. The experiments are simple and easy to do, yet they are *real* science experiments that help students develop the skills they need for *real* scientific investigations.

Each experiment is one page and contains a short objective, the materials needed, a brief outline of the experiment, and any graphics or illustrations needed to enhance the experiment. The skill being explored is listed in the upper right-hand corner of each page.

The *Super Simple Science Experiments Laboratory Notebook* is a companion book for use with these experiments. It includes lined pages, blank pages, and graphing pages, providing students with a place to record their experimental data in different formats.

Getting Started

Below is a list of the materials and equipment needed for all of the biology experiments in this book. You can collect most of the materials ahead of time and place them in a storage bin or drawer.

Materials at a Glance

Foods

beans, dried (3)
bread slices (2)
celery stalks with leaves (2)
pectin or Jell-O (2 boxes)
meat tenderizer
onion
paper towel
raw egg
salt
sprig of mint
sugar
water, distilled
water, tap

Materials

*Super Simple Science Experiments
    Laboratory Notebook*
balloons (several)
candle, small
cotton swabs
drinking straw
food coloring
insects (dead or alive)
liquid detergent
marble
marking pen
matches
paper (shredded newspaper or
    office paper)
paper, white absorbent
pencil
plant or animal to observe
plastic sealable bags (small, clear)
plastic wrap
redworms, composting (Eisenia
    fetida) - .25 kg (1/2 lb.)
rock
rubber band
rubbing alcohol
spiders (dead or alive)
tape
water: pond water, hay water, or
    filtered water & soil mixture

Equipment

binoculars
blender
container, large, for water
cooking pan
jars, clear glass (2)
magnifying glass
measuring cup
measuring spoons
microscope & depression
    slides
petri dish or large jar top
refrigerator
scissors
storage bin, plastic with
    holes
stove
strainer
test tube or narrow jar,
    clear
tongs

Other

area with plants (garden, park, forest, etc.)
anthill with ant trail
area frequented by birds

Resources

computer with internet access, encyclopedia,
    or library

Laboratory Safety

Most of these experiments use household items. Extra care should be taken while working with blenders, stoves, and matches in this series of experiments. The following are some general laboratory precautions that should be applied to the home laboratory:

Never put things in your mouth without explicit instructions to do so. This means that food items should not be eaten unless tasting or eating is part of the experiment.

Use safety glasses while working with glass objects or strong chemicals such as bleach.

Wash hands before and after handling chemicals.

Use adult supervision while conducting any step requiring a blender, a stove, or matches.

Table of Contents

1. What Is Life?

Objective

To observe the differences between living and non-living things.

Materials

pencil
rock
a plant or animal that can be observed
Super Simple Science Experiments
    Laboratory Notebook

Questions

❶ Place the rock on a table or other flat surface. While observing the rock, answer the following questions in your laboratory notebook.

  ① Does the rock move on its own?
  ② Does the rock require any food to exist?
  ③ Can the rock reproduce itself, creating little rocks?

❷ Observe any plant or animal and answer the following questions in your laboratory notebook.
  ① Does the plant or animal move on its own?
  ② Does the plant or animal require any food to exist?
  ③ Can the plant or animal reproduce itself, creating little plants or animals?

Results and Conclusions

The first step in studying life is to understand the difference between something that is "alive" and something that is "not alive." However, defining life can be challenging. Based on your observations, how would you define "life?" Are there any other aspects of life that distinguish living things from non-living things?

2. The Chemistry of Life

using resources

Objective

To observe the differences between the chemistry of living and non-living things.

Materials

pencil
internet resources or encyclopedia
Super Simple Science Experiments
    Laboratory Notebook

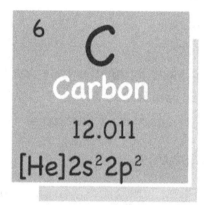

Experiment

❶ Research the elements carbon and silicon using the internet or an encyclopedia and answer the following questions. Record your answers in your laboratory notebook.

① How many bonds do carbon and silicon typically form?
② Is CO_2 a gas or solid at room temperature?
③ Is SiO_2 a gas or a solid at room temperature?
④ Which are stronger, Si-Si bonds or C-C bonds?

Results and Conclusions

Living things such as plants and animals are carbon-based. Non-living things such as rocks are silicon-based. Although both carbon and silicon can form the same number of bonds, compounds made with silicon are very different from compounds made with carbon. How do you think the difference between the chemistry of carbon and the chemistry of silicon creates the differences we observe between living and non-living things?

3. Proteins Make Life Possible

Objective

To observe what happens when proteins are heated.

Materials

pencil
raw egg
cooking pan
Super Simple Science Experiments Laboratory Notebook

Experiment

❶ Crack open a raw egg and pour its contents into a cooking pan. Observe the color and texture of the egg, and record your observations in your laboratory notebook.

❷ Heat the cooking pan slowly. Observe how the egg changes. Record your observations in your laboratory notebook.

❸ Place the egg in a refrigerator and let the egg cool to its original temperature. Observe whether or not the egg is able to return to its original condition when it has cooled. Record your observations in your laboratory notebook.

❹ Answer the following questions in your laboratory notebook.

①   Do you think the egg is "alive" before you crack it open? (if it is a fresh egg that is fertilized, can it grow into a chick?) Why or why not?

②   Do you think the egg is "alive" after you crack it open and heat it in the pan? Why or why not?

③   Do you think the egg can go back to being "alive" when it has cooled? Why or why not?

Results and Conclusions

Some of the most essential molecules in living thing are proteins. A fertilized egg is able to develop into a full-grown chicken because of the "protein machines" inside the yolk. However, if the egg is opened and the contents heated, the protein machines are destroyed. The proteins cannot be repaired, and the egg is no longer "alive."

4. Simple DNA Extraction

using techniques

Objective

To use a DNA extraction technique to remove DNA from an onion.

Materials

1 onion	strainer
blender	liquid detergent
salt	measuring cup & measuring spoons
water	clear test tube or narrow jar
meat tenderizer	drinking straw
rubbing alcohol	*Super Simple Science Experiments Laboratory Notebook*

Experiment

❶ Place the onion in the blender and add 237 ml (1 cup) of cold water and .6 ml (1/8 teaspoon) of salt.

❷ Blend on high until the onion is liquefied.

❸ Pour the onion-water-salt mixture through a strainer and into a measuring cup to remove any large chunks of onion.

❹ Add 30 ml (2 tablespoons) of liquid detergent and swirl to mix. Allow the mixture to sit for 15 minutes.

❺ Carefully transfer 60 ml (1/4 cup) of the mixture to a clear test tube or narrow jar.

❻ Add a pinch of meat tenderizer and stir gently.

❼ Tilt the jar and slowly add rubbing alcohol. The alcohol will float on top of the onion mixture. You should see stringy white clumps form.

❽ Using the straw, gently pull the white clumps away from the mixture. This is DNA. Record your observations in your laboratory notebook.

Results and Conclusions

All living things contain DNA. DNA stands for deoxyribonucleic acid. DNA is the "code" that tells cells how to grow, when to divide, and when to die. Try repeating the experiment using raw spinach, green peas, pinto beans, or other foods. Do all of these contain DNA? Repeat the experiment using a non-living item like sand, but for Steps 1 and 2, instead of using a blender, make the mixture in a container and stir it. What are your results?

5. How Plants Breathe

Objective

To observe that plants give off oxygen during photosynthesis.

Materials

pencil
glass jar
small candle
matches
sprig of mint
Super Simple Science Experiments
    Laboratory Notebook

Experiment

❶ Light the candle and observe how it burns.

❷ Place the glass jar upside down over the candle and carefully observe what happens. Repeat this several times and note how long it takes for the flame to extinguish.

❸ Light the candle again and place the sprig of mint next to it (without contacting the flame!). Place the glass jar over the burning candle and the mint sprig, and carefully observe how long it takes for the flame to extinguish.

❹ Record your observations in your laboratory notebook.

Results and Conclusions

In 1771, using a candle, a jar, and a sprig of mint, Joseph Priestley discovered that plants release oxygen. This famous but simple experiment paved the way for understanding the cellular process of photosynthesis. During photosynthesis, plants take up carbon dioxide from the air and release oxygen. Priestley observed that a candle will burn longer in the presence of a sprig of mint. From this observation, he concluded that plants release "something" (that we now know is oxygen) into the air, allowing a candle to burn longer under a glass jar.

6. Do Plants Drink at Night?

Objective

To observe whether or not capillary action in plants depends on light.

Materials

2 celery stalks with leaves
food coloring
2 jars
Super Simple Science Experiments Laboratory Notebook

Experiment

❶ Cut the blunt end off both celery stalks. Don't cut off the leaves.
❷ Place each celery stalk in a jar with 118 ml (1/2 cup) cup of water.
❸ Add several drops of food coloring to the water in each jar. Swirl.
❹ Place one stalk in a brightly lit room and the other in a dark room.
❺ Allow the stalks to sit for an hour.
❻ Record your observations in your laboratory notebook.

Results and Conclusions

When you drink through a straw, you are using capillary action. Plants also use capillary action when they pull water upward from their roots.

In order for capillary action to work with a straw, both ends of the straw need to be open. The same is true for plants. Plants have microscopic pores on their surface that open in the early morning light and close at night. The experimental control or "normal" activity of capillary action is observed in the celery stalk placed in the light. By comparing the control to the capillary action of a celery stalk placed in the dark, the effect of light on capillary action in plants can be directly observed.

7. Model of a Cell

Objective

To understand how a cell membrane holds cellular material together.

Materials

pencil
small plastic sealable bag
pectin or Jell-O
marble
Super Simple Science Experiments Laboratory Notebook

Experiment

❶ Make a stiff pectin or Jell-O mixture following the instructions on the box.

❷ When the mixture has cooled enough to touch, partially fill the small plastic sealable bag with the mixture. Add the marble and seal the bag. Maneuver the marble until it rests in the center of the bag.

❸ Allow the mixture to cool and jell in the refrigerator.

❹ When the mixture has cooled, observe how the bag and its contents behave. Notice how the bag holds the contents together and how the marble stays towards the center of the bag even as you rotate the bag in your hands.

❺ Record your observations in your laboratory notebook.

Results and Conclusions

In many ways a cell is similar to a bag full of Jell-O. A cell membrane holds the contents of the cell together. Inside the cell is the cytoplasm. The cytoplasm is made mostly of water but also has a highly intricate and organized network of molecules. The cellular matrix allows small molecules and ions to move freely while keeping larger structures, such as the cell nucleus, in place.

Cross section of a cell

8. Protozoa

observation

Objective

To observe microscopic protozoa in pond water.

Materials

microscope
depression slides
pond water (alternatively, use hay water or
    water and soil mixed and filtered)
Super Simple Science Experiments
    Laboratory Notebook

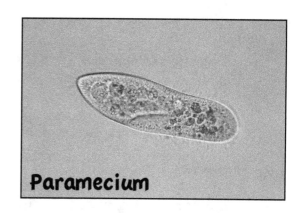

Paramecium

Experiment

❶ Place a drop of pond water on a slide.
❷ Observe the pond water using the 10x or 40x power on the microscope.
❸ Record your observations in your laboratory notebook.

Results and Conclusions

Protozoa are tiny single-celled organisms that can be found almost everywhere. Protozoa are remarkable in that they can eat, digest, move, and respond to external stimuli all within a single cell. Protozoa come in many different shapes and sizes and move in a variety of ways. Pond water, hay water, and soil water contain many different kinds of protozoa. How many different protozoa can you observe? Is there a difference between pond water, hay water, and soil water?

9. Bacteria

Objective

To test for bacteria.

Materials

box of gelatin or pectin
sugar
petri dish (or pickle jar top and
    wax paper)
distilled water
cooking pot
measuring cup, measuring spoons, and tongs
cotton swab
Super Simple Science Experiments Laboratory Notebook

Experiment

❶ Sterilize the petri dish or pickle jar tops by boiling in hot water for 10 minutes. Remove with tongs and set aside to cool.

❷ Boil 60 ml (1/4 cup) of water and add 5 ml (1 teaspoon) of gelatin and 5 ml (1 teaspoon) of sugar. Cook one minute or until gelatin and sugar are dissolved.

❸ Fill the petri dish or pickle jar top to a little below the top edge. Immediately place the cover on the petri dish or wax paper on the pickle jar top. Allow to cool.

❹ Wet the cotton swab with distilled water, and then wipe any surface such as a door knob, computer keyboard, toilet bowl, or kitchen sink. Wipe the swab on the solid gelatin mixture. Keep at room temperature for several days.

❺ Record your observations in your laboratory notebook.

Results and Conclusions

Bacteria are microscopic organisms found everywhere. Many bacteria live on surfaces. Some bacteria cause disease in humans, and some are beneficial. Because bacteria are living things, they require food to survive. Bacteria will multiply and grow on a medium such as gelatin with sugar. What happens if you make the gelatin without sugar or place your petri dish in a cold environment? Do the bacteria still grow?

10. Bread Mold

observation
using controls

Objective

To observe the growth of mold on bread.

Materials

2 slices of bread
2 clear, sealable plastic sandwich bags
marking pen
Super Simple Science Experiments
   Laboratory Notebook

Experiment

❶ Allow the bread slices to sit in the open for half an hour. Then place each slice in a separate sealable plastic bag. Label the bags A and B.
❷ Add a few drops of water to each bag and seal.
❸ Place bag A in a warm, dark place. Place bag B in the refrigerator.
❹ Allow the bags to sit for one to two weeks.
❺ Record your observations in your laboratory notebook.
❻ Do not open sealed mold bags before discarding.

Results and Conclusions

Bread mold is a type of fungus that grows in warm, moist environments. Unlike plants, molds don't grow from seeds but rather from spores that float in the air. Cold temperatures slow the growth of bread mold. Although some molds can cause disease in humans, molds provide a necessary step in the cycle of life. Molds help foods rot by breaking down organic matter, turning it into slime. As a result, molds make nutrients available for new plants.

11. Roots and Shoots

Objective

To observe the directional growth of roots and shoots produced by a bean.

Materials

3 dried beans
white absorbent paper
scissors
clear glass jar
water
plastic wrap
rubber band
Super Simple Science Experiments Laboratory Notebook

Experiment

❶ Cut the white paper lengthwise so that it will fit around the inside of the glass jar.

❷ Moisten the paper and place it around the inside of the jar.

❸ Place three beans in different orientations (up, down, and sideways) between the paper and the jar. This will gently hold the beans in place.

❹ Fill the bottom of the jar with clean water, allowing the water to contact the white paper and being careful not to submerge the beans. Gently cover the jar with plastic wrap and secure it with a rubber band.

❺ Allow the jar to sit for several days. Observe when the beans first start to sprout. Note the direction in which the roots and shoots are growing. Record your observations in your laboratory notebook.

Results and Conclusions

Seeds "know" in which direction to grow their roots and shoots. This "knowing" is possible because of a biological phenomenon called tropism. Tropism means "a turning," and plants can direct their growth toward or away from various external factors, such as sunlight or gravity. Seeds direct their roots downward toward the center of the Earth using gravitational tropism. They grow their shoots upward toward the Sun using phototropism.

12. Nature Walk—Plant Classification

Objective

To observe the difference between monocot and dicot plants.

Materials

pencil
a garden, park, forest, or other area
    where plants can be observed
Super Simple Science Experiments
    Laboratory Notebook

	Monocot	Dicot
Seeds	single cotyledon	double cotyledon
Leaves	parallel veins	branched veins
Flowers	multiples of 3	multiples of 5
Roots	fibrous root	tap root

Experiment

❶ Take a walk in a place where you can observe several different kinds of plants.

❷ In your laboratory notebook, illustrate (to the best of your ability) the leaves, flowers, and roots of different plants.

❸ Using the criteria in the table, determine if the plant is a monocot or a dicot.

❹ If you know the name of the plant, record it next to the illustration you drew.

❺ Look up as many plants as you can, using the internet, encyclopedia, field guide, or other reference. Determine if your analysis is correct.

Results and Conclusions

By carefully observing seeds, leaves, flowers, and roots, you can determine if a plant is a monocot or a dicot. How many monocots did you observe? How many dicots? What about plants that don't have flowers or produce pine cones? How do you think these are classified?

13. Worm Test

Objective

To test the hypothesis that redworms can recycle paper.

Materials

.25 kilogram (1/2 pound) of composting
    redworms (Eisenia fetida)
shredded newspaper or office paper
plastic storage bin with holes
water
*Super Simple Science Experiments
    Laboratory Notebook*

Experiment

❶ Place the shredded newspaper or office paper in the bin. Add enough water to make the paper damp but not wet.

❷ Add the composting redworms and keep in a moderately warm place. Keep the shredded paper damp but not wet.

❸ Observe your worms for several weeks and record your observations in your laboratory notebook.

Results and Conclusions

Worms are decomposers and live on dead organic matter. Many types of paper contain carbohydrates, and finding ways to naturally convert paper back to essential nutrients for soil is important. Were the worms able to survive on paper alone?

*To find sources for redworms, do an internet search on Eisenia fetida

14. Ants

Objective

To observe what happens when an ant trail is disrupted.

Materials

ant trail
pencil
Super Simple Science Experiments
    Laboratory Notebook

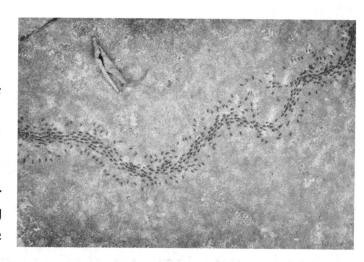

Experiment

❶ Go outside and find an anthill. Observe any ant trails leading away from the anthill. (Avoid fire ants if they are in your area.)

❷ Follow the ant trail to its end, if possible. Observe how the ants move through the trail. Write down as many details as possible in your laboratory notebook.

❸ Carefully disrupt the trail by gently washing away a portion of the trail with clean water. Be careful not to drown the ants.

❹ Observe the ants after the disruption. Were the ants able to recover their trail? If so, how did they do this? Record your observations in your laboratory notebook.

Results and Conclusions

Ants work in communities and are able to efficiently communicate with each other by using chemicals called pheromones. When one ant finds food, she leaves a trail of pheromones to signal other ants to follow her. Washing away the pheromones will cause a disruption in the trail. However, many times ants can re-establish their trail.

15. Insects and Spiders

Objective

To compare body plans between insects and spiders.

Materials

insects (dead or alive), such as
    ants, beetles, butterflies, etc.
spiders (dead or alive)
magnifying glass
shallow dish or jar with holes in
    the cover
*Super Simple Science Experiments
    Laboratory Notebook*

Experiment

❶ If you are using live insects, place them in a shallow dish or in a jar with holes in the cover. If you are using dead insects, place them several inches apart on a white sheet of paper.

❷ Observe the insects with your magnifying glass. Look for the number of legs, number of antennae, and number of body segments. Note any other interesting features. Record your observations in your laboratory notebook

❸ Place live spiders in the shallow dish or a jar, or dead spiders on a piece of white paper.

❹ Observe the spiders with your magnifying glass. Look for the number of legs, number of antennae, and number of body segments. Note any other interesting features. Record your observations in your laboratory notebook.

Results and Conclusions

Spiders are often confused with insects because from a distance they look very similar. However, spiders are not insects and have a distinctly different body plan.

16. Jellyfish

observation

Objective

To create a model jellyfish and explore how a jellyfish moves.

Materials

paper towel
scissors
tape
water in a large container
Super Simple Science Experiments
    Laboratory Notebook

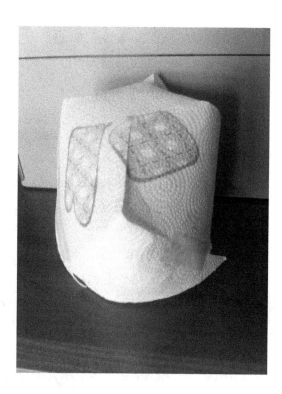

Experiment

❶ Use a square paper towel or cut the paper towel into a square using scissors.

❷ Cut a slit from each of the four corners of the paper towel halfway to the center of the paper towel.

❸ Lap the edges of each slit over each other and tape in place, creating a small dome.

❹ Place the dome in water and move it up and down. Observe how the water fills the dome and how pulling up on the paper towel collapses the dome. Record your observations in your laboratory notebook.

Results and Conclusions

A jellyfish is not a true fish but an organism that has no external or internal skeleton. The body of a jellyfish is supported by the surrounding water, and a jellyfish moves by pulling water in and expelling water out of its soft body.

17. Birds

Objective

To observe birds in flight.

Materials

binoculars
nearby park, open space, or public building
    frequented by birds
Super Simple Science Experiments
    Laboratory Notebook

Experiment

❶ Find a place in a nearby park, open space, or
    public building where you can watch birds.
❷ Using the binoculars, observe the birds and
    how they fly.
❸ Try to notice how a bird takes off, lands, climbs, or glides.
❹ Observe any differences between small birds, large birds, and hummingbirds. Record
    your observations in your laboratory notebook.

Results and Conclusions

Bird flight is an amazing feat of engineering. Many birds can take off from a standing
position, hover, land without a runway, climb to great heights, glide, and dive. Bird
bones are lightweight yet strong, and a bird's wing is aerodynamically designed to
create lift force.

18. Reptiles

Objective

To model how a reptile regulates body temperature.

Materials

several balloons
water
Super Simple Science Experiments
    Laboratory Notebook

Experiment

❶ Fill several balloons with water and tie
    them off.

❷ Place the balloons outside in several locations. Choose a few locations where the
    balloons will receive direct sunlight and a few locations where the balloons will
    remain in the shade.

❸ With your hands, note the initial general temperature of your balloons (hot, warm,
    cool, cold). In your laboratory notebook record the general temperature and the
    location of each balloon.

❹ Allow the balloons to sit for several hours outside and then feel each balloon with
    your hands. Record the temperature of each balloon in your laboratory notebook and
    note if the temperature has changed.

❺ Move the balloons to new locations and repeat step ❸ and ❹.

Results and Conclusions

Reptiles are exothermic, or "cold blooded," meaning they are not able to regulate their
body temperature internally. Because they are exothermic, a reptile's body temperature
will change with its surroundings. Reptiles cool down in the shade and warm up in the
sun. Reptiles will hibernate in the winter months because it is too cold for their bodies
to work properly. In the summer months, they will warm themselves by sitting on warm
rocks or in direct sunlight.

19. Mammals

Objective

To use resources for researching mammals.

Materials

internet, encyclopedia, or local library
Super Simple Science Experiments Laboratory Notebook

Experiment

❶ Write the following animal names across the top of several pieces of paper or in your laboratory notebook:

platypus, porcupine, aardvark, bat, wolf, tiger, whale, mouse, cow, elephant, rabbit

❷ Below each animal's name answer the following questions:

① What does the mammal eat?

② Does the mammal bear live young, or does it lay eggs?

③ Does the mammal have fur or hair?

④ Does the mammal breathe with lungs?

⑤ Does the mammal live on land, in the water, or both?

❸ In your laboratory notebook answer the following questions:

① Are all mammals the same?

② Do all mammals have fur or hair?

③ Do all mammals bear live young?

④ Do all mammals use lungs to breathe?

Results and Conclusions

Mammals are a broad group of living things that share some common features but are not all the same. Mammals share some features that distinguish them from other groups of animals. Based on your research, what is a mammal?

20. Humans

Objective

To learn about humans by observing the self.

Materials

yourself
Super Simple Science Experiments
    Laboratory Notebook

Experiment

❶ You are a human and can observe yourself to learn more about humans.

❷ In your laboratory notebook answer the following questions:

① What do you eat?

② How often do you need to eat and how do you know you need to eat?

③ Describe how you walk.

④ Describe how you breathe.

⑤ Does your body temperature stay the same (unless you have a fever)?

⑥ When do you sleep and for how long?

⑦ Feel your pulse. How does your heart beat?

⑧ How are you reading, writing, and thinking right now?

Results and Conclusions

Humans have many unique features that distinguish them from other animals. For example, humans are the only mammals that are bipedal and can walk upright. Humans are also the only mammals that have the cognitive capacity for complex language and the ability to create art, write novels, or use advanced technology.

21. Connections

Objective

To observe some of the many different connections we have to other living things.

Materials

yourself
*Super Simple Science Experiments
  Laboratory Notebook*

Experiment

❶ You are connected to many different types of life in many different ways.

❷ In your laboratory notebook answer the following questions:

① Where does your food come from?

② Where does your oxygen come from?

③ If you have pets, describe them and how you interact with them.

④ Describe the insects that live near your house and sometimes visit inside.

⑤ Describe all the animal sounds you hear when you walk on the street, in a park, or in a forest.

⑥ How do living things help with farming, transportation, or digestion?

⑦ How do we help or harm other living things?

Results and Conclusions

All of life is interconnected. Plants, animals, and microorganisms play a significant role in our everyday lives, and we play a role in their lives. The air we breathe, the food we eat, and the way we digest our food are all affected by other living things. Observing these connections is the first step toward understanding how biology works in our everyday lives.

More REAL SCIENCE-4-KIDS Books
by Rebecca W. Keller, PhD

Focus Series unit study program — each title has a Student Textbook with accompanying Laboratory Workbook, Teacher's Manual, Study Folder, Quizzes, and Recorded Lectures

Focus On Elementary Chemistry
Focus On Elementary Biology
Focus On Elementary Physics
Focus On Elementary Geology
Focus On Elementary Astronomy

Focus On Middle School Chemistry
Focus On Middle School Biology
Focus On Middle School Physics
Focus On Middle School Geology
Focus On Middle School Astronomy

Focus On High School Chemistry

Building Blocks Series yearlong study program — each Student Textbook has accompanying Laboratory Notebook, Teacher's Manual, Lesson Plan, and Quizzes

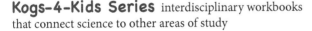

Exploring the Building Blocks of Science Book K (Activity Book)
Exploring the Building Blocks of Science Book 1
Exploring the Building Blocks of Science Book 2
Exploring the Building Blocks of Science Book 3
Exploring the Building Blocks of Science Book 4
Exploring the Building Blocks of Science Book 5
Exploring the Building Blocks of Science Book 6
Exploring the Building Blocks of Science Book 7
Exploring the Building Blocks of Science Book 8

Super Simple Science Experiments Series

21 Super Simple Chemistry Experiments
21 Super Simple Biology Experiments
21 Super Simple Physics Experiments
21 Super Simple Geology Experiments
21 Super Simple Astronomy Experiments
101 Super Simple Science Experiments

Kogs-4-Kids Series interdisciplinary workbooks that connect science to other areas of study

Physics Connects to Language
Biology Connects to Language
Chemistry Connects to Language
Geology Connects to Language
Astronomy Connects to Language

Note: A few titles may still be in production.

Gravitas Publications Inc.

www.realscience4kids.com

GRAVITAS
PUBLICATIONS

CPSIA information can be obtained
at www.ICGtesting.com
Printed in the USA
LVHW102032160419
614427LV00001B/6/P